MW01291762

think upside down™

The Avatars of Eden

bringing

Heaven

to

Earth

Aliyah Marr

This book and other products to aid creative development may be ordered directly from the publisher at:

www.parallelmindzz.com *The Playground for Creative Minds*

Marr, Aliyah

The Avatars of Eden: Bringing Heaven to Earth / Aliyah Marr—1st ed.
ISBN-13: 978-1537749266
ISBN-10: 1537749269

1. Ascension 2. Avatar Movie 3. 5th dimension 4. Indigos 5. Lightworkers 6. Starseeds 7. Indigos 8. Ancient Mysteries

Table of Contents

Caveat

The ideas presented in this book may seem outlandish, irrational, and improbable to you. They may challenge your most cherished beliefs or they may suddenly put things in a new perspective.

On the other hand, you may choose to see this book as pure fiction. Perhaps it's best to see the ideas presented here as a parable about evolution and consciousness—a tale of how a planet evolves and how consciousness creates drama, polarity, and variety in order to know itself.

**D**edication

To my mother, who taught me to love and honor my Mother.

The Way of Love

Simple, gracious, Lovely in itself

Love comes in unexpected moments

Slips inside like the hand of a small child

Love is trust in the moment

Tiny and large at the same time

Love is without expectations

Love is without desire

Love is requited and never wanting

Love is a garden of never-ending delight

Love is all sensation

Love is consumed by the eyes

Love is held in the heart

Love is the only thing that can be multiplied

And divided endlessly.

– Aliyah Marr, September 11, 2008

Preface

This book is the sequel to a book I wrote in 2014, called *Unplug From the Matrix*, which depicted a Matrix-like world of domination and control.

The *Avatars of Eden* proposes an alternative vision; a future of peace, harmony, and abundance for all, embedded in our minds as the ancient legend of Eden.

Prologue

Neytiri: Our great mother does not take sides, she protects the balance of life.

The Enduring Legend of Eden
The ancient legend of Eden is based upon an older universal myth, an idyllic place of timeless beauty, a Paradise, sometimes called the Otherworld. In ancient Egypt, it was called Aaru, the reed-fields of ideal hunting and fishing grounds where the dead lived after judgment. The Fortunate Isle of Mag Mell was the Paradise of the Celts. In ancient Greece, it was the Elysian fields; a land of plenty where the heroic and righteous dead hoped to spend eternity. The Eden of the British Isles was an island named Avalon. In Tibetan Buddhism it is called Shambala; a core concept that describes a realm of harmony between man and nature, connected with the Kalachakra or "wheel of time.

Eden Foretold
Every culture describes their version of Eden as a place of peace and plenitude. This story is a universal archetype that tells us that we once lived in harmony with nature, and can do so again. All the legends agree on one thing: Eden isn't just a story from the remote past, Eden is our destiny.

Chapter I

Illusion and Illumination

~ 11 ~

Dr. Grace Augustine: You know, they never even wanted us to succeed. They bulldoze sacred sites on purpose, to trigger a response. They are fabricating this war to get what they want.

Jake Sully: This is how it's done. When people are sitting on shit that you want, you make them your enemy. Then you're justified in taking it.

Avatar

The movie *Avatar* is set on a densely forested moon called Pandora which orbits a star in the Alpha Centauri system. Pandora is inhabited by the Na'vi, blue-skinned humanoids who live in harmony with nature and worship a mother goddess called Eywa.

To explore this world, whose atmosphere is poisonous to humans, scientists create environmentally-adapted bodies called "avatars," which can be remote-controlled by the mind of a human.

1

Picturing Eden

Avatar's story centers around a conflict between humans from Earth who want to mine Pandora and the natives who live there. The film depicts 22nd century Earth as a world with an enslaved populace and a ravished ecosystem; the results of a system of governance and values that emphasize profit at the expense of the planet and the people. As the film's hero Jake Sully says, "There's no green there, they killed their Mother." In contrast, Pandora is a veritable Eden, and the Na'vi as beings who live in harmony with nature.

> *The Na'vi represent something that is our higher selves, or our aspirational selves, what we would like to think we are and that, even though there are good humans within the film, the humans represent what we know to be the parts of ourselves that are trashing our world and maybe condemning ourselves to a grim future.*[1]

The Underpinnings of the Matrix

In *The Avatars of Eden* the phrase, "the Matrix" refers to Earth's current system of control and domination. Like the grid of a giant holodeck,[2] the Matrix projects a fantasy which we have come to believe is real. The Matrix is fueled by our beliefs and emotions.

---

1 *Avatar* Director James Cameron

2 A holodeck is a fictional virtual reality device in the *Star Trek* series.

From the day we are born, the Matrix force-feeds us ideas that are designed to keep us in the Matrix. As our thoughts create our reality, the Matrix sustains and recreates itself by directing those thoughts and telling us what to believe.

You are indoctrinated with many thoughts, beliefs, and "facts" that pertain to the Matrix, but do not benefit or support you. These beliefs run invisibly in the background; they are unnatural to your innate Self, but they are drilled inexorably into your brain day after day, until you accept them. We are all subject to this conditioning; it is what finally kills us in the end.

A core belief is invisible only when you think of it as a fact of life, and not as a belief about life... you must become aware of your own structures. Build them up or tear them down, but do not allow yourself to become blind to the furniture of your own mind... it will help you, in fact, if you think of your own beliefs as furniture that can be rearranged, changed, renewed, completely discarded or replaced.

Your ideas are yours. They should not control you. Imagine yourself then rearranging this furniture. Images of particular pieces will come clearly to you. Ask yourself what ideas these pieces represent. See how well the tables fit together. Open up the drawers inside.

You must understand that these are not simply dead ideas, like debris, within your mind. They are psychic matter. In a sense then they are alive. They group themselves like cells, protecting their own validity and identity. You feed them, figuratively speaking, with like ideas.[1]

The Origins of Fear

An individual cannot leave the Matrix until he transcends the belief system that supports it. That belief system is fueled by the emotion of FEAR. Fear comes from an incomplete worldview: a limited perspective. A small child who is suddenly separated from his mother in a crowd becomes fearful. This is because the child has the lower perspective of separation. If the child could see the whole crowd from above, he would see his mother looking for him, and realize that he is only temporarily separated.

When you have an inclusive, unlimited holistic view, you cannot experience fear because you are at a higher perspective. It is only in the state of separation and limitation that fear can exist.

The Secret Desire of Fear

Fear cannot be conquered by fear; it must be conquered by love. An old episode of "Star Trek Voyager" shows how.

---

1 "The Seth Material." Roberts, Jane. Bantam. 1976.

The Voyager crew found a number of people on a planet imprisoned in stasis, who had failed to wake up four years earlier as originally scheduled. The crew finds out that the minds of the people in hibernation were kept active inside a virtual reality run by a computer. Something had gone horribly wrong: instead of providing a pleasant holographic environment for the people in stasis, the computer generated a circus filled with characters that tortured them with fears generated by their own imaginations.

Their minds were kept eternally awake in a virtual circus-like world dominated by a clown character named Fear. The people in stasis had not woken up on schedule, and in fact, two of the five had died of massive heart attacks brought on by the extreme stress generated by the circus of fear.

To rescue her people and the aliens caught within this world, Captain Kathryn Janeway projects a hologram of herself as a substitute hostage. Fear doesn't know that Janeway is a hologram, and therefore not subject to the environment or the characters in the virtual circus of fear. He is relishing the prospect of torturing someone of Janeway's caliber and is willing to give up all the others in exchange for her. He is highly entertained by the idea of someone "choosing" to be with him. But when Fear finds out that Janeway is just a projection like him, he begins to become afraid, knowing that he cannot exist without a mind to live within.

Janeway tells him that she knows his secret desire: she knows that Fear wants to be conquered.

Fear needs to surrender to Love. But because Fear, knowing only hatred, battle, war, and separation, cannot understand the higher concept of surrender, it has to be "conquered"—as if it is in a battle—by Love.

Fear exists to be defeated; the entire purpose of its existence is to experience love through the unimaginable act of surrender. Fear unconsciously desires to be reunited with its polar opposite Love. In doing so, Fear achieves its real goal; surrendering in order that it may become whole.

"I'm afraid," Fear says just before he dissolves.

Janeway whispers, "I know."[1]

Overcoming the False Premise

The central premise of separation spawns a number of other false premises.

One is the premise of lack. This is patently false, as the universe is abundantly abundant. It is so cleverly

---

1 First published in 2011 in parallelmind.wordpress.com

abundant that it can also be abundant in lack. Like a Chinese embroidery where every millimeter of space is occupied with an image, so our universe is filled to the brim. We have learned to believe in lack and so we close our eyes to the natural abundance that surrounds us.

Another false premise is the belief in the absence of love. It is everywhere; in the very air we breathe and in the water we drink. Gaia is love; we are love. Everything is an expression of love.

Fall from Grace

And so, in the Eden of the eternal now, dropped the stone of false belief, called FEAR, shattering the Eternal Now and fracturing the experience of Being into the realization of Time.

The traumatic effects of this identity-smashing event has haunted humanity with a deep feeling of loss, culpability, and shame for untold generations.

A fragmented god litters the surface of the Earth, present but hidden in all the pieces of his original creation; in the plants and animals, which man came to exploit and abuse in his grief and ignorance. The fragments of the original truth still lie on the ground, and as man views himself through the shards of the mirror, he sees only an irreparable tragedy; the loss of his wholeness and the shattering of Heaven, reflected as pieces that he can no longer interpret or feel. Once he lost his sense of the whole, he became "mortal"—a being that has forgot that he is the god he longs for.

Incarnating into the Matrix

When you incarnated on this Earth plane, you split your original energy into three parts:

> 1: Higher Self / Super Conscious
> 2: Mental Body / Ego / Self-Conscious
> 3: Subconscious / Emotional & Physical Body

When this split happened, several conditions or issues emerged:

1. Descent into the lower vibrational reality of the Matrix required that you forget the Higher Reality outside; you had to forget the greater reality of Love.

2. The Matrix inserted a new base level of programming in the Self-Conscious: the experience of separation and limitation.

3. The experience of separation engenders fear. Fear puts us into "survival mode" which cuts off the higher functioning of the brain, and keeps us in the lower vibration of the Matrix. Fear does not exist in the larger reality outside, since separation does not exist. Fear is an essential part of duality.

4. Duality is a system that always seeks equilibrium. Like algebra, one side of the equation has to equal the other

side. Karma developed to create balance over time, thus "an eye for an eye, a tooth for a tooth" became the primary thinking on the planet. In a space-time continuum, cause and effect can be separated by time.

5. Fear traps us in the Matrix by creating resistance. Resistance is a natural brake to the flow of desire: it creates time, which gives us more experience. Since the law of resonance requires that the vibration of our "exterior" reality match our internal vibration, fear-based thoughts and emotions keep us imprisoned in the Matrix, while higher vibrational thoughts and feelings allow us to "escape" it.

The apparent freedom and self-assertion of our personal being to which we are so profoundly attached, conceal a most pitiable subjection to a thousand suggestions, impulsions, forces which we have made extraneous to your little person. Our ego, boasting of freedom, is at every moment the slave, toy and puppet of countless beings, powers, forces, influences in universal Nature.

All life is the play of universal forces. The individual gives a personal form to these universal forces. But he can choose whether he shall respond or not to the action of a particular force. Only most people do not really choose – they indulge the play of the forces. Your illnesses, depressions, etc. are the repeated play of such forces. It is only

when one can make oneself free of them that one
can be the true person and have a true life—but
one can be free only by living in the Divine.[1]

Paradise Lost

Eons ago, we were thrown into the Matrix of fear. Surviving became a matter of exploiting nature, killing others for land, and amassing more and more wealth. In order to ensure their safety, individuals endeavored to climb the rungs of the hierarchy. If it meant murder, rape, abuse, exploitation, war, racism, and prejudice, we accepted that the ends justified the means; in the Matrix, our personal survival and wellbeing were paramount. We came to accept that these negative qualities were "natural" for mankind and that "survival of the fittest" was the reality of the planet.

The Fall into the Land of Belief caused Earth to spin like an unbalanced top into a spiral of descending consciousness. Lacking connection with our original selves and thrust outside the truth of our physical bodies and hearts, we lost our connection with the divine feminine —Eden— which had nourished our physical, emotional, and creative selves for so long. This was very traumatic for mankind. We carry a wound in our bodies and in our minds from untold eons of survival conditions, violence, and fear.

We lost Paradise when we lost connection with the eternal NOW, and fell into a dream of time and space. When we lost our respect for life; we lost our connection with the

---

1 "The Hidden Forces of Life," Sri Aurobindo

Earth, and, eventually, we lost touch with our own divine nature. This unnatural and unbalanced belief system threw us out of the higher dimensional reality of Eden.

The Paradise that we lost is in another layer of reality— very close to this one. It has been there all along, through all our troubles, trials, and tribulations; it is just within reach. A shiver of a vibration, a conscious choice, and we are back in Paradise.

Chapter II

The Master Builder

~ 22 ~

Moat: It is decided. My daughter will teach you our ways. Learn well, Jake Sully, and we will see if your insanity can be cured.

There are no Materialists in Eden

The legend of Eden has survived into modern times, despite the power of the materialists. "Materialists" are those who focus solely upon material existence. They are the "global elite" who created the hierarchy of the Matrix. In this system, everyone is assigned a value and a position of relative power; the materialists place themselves at the top and everyone else below them.

The best propaganda is invisible. Like a drip of water that slowly forms a stalagmite on the floor of a dark cave, the propaganda of the materialists accrues invisibly over time. They promote the idea that man's innate nature is greedy, violent, and selfish: most people accept that this is how things are and will always be.

When a belief system is in place for a long time, it becomes an unquestioned and invisible "truth" in the minds of the populace. The materialists' description of man makes it easy for them to control us by justifying a social system that violates all natural laws. It allows them to rape and pillage to their hearts' content, knowing that they are hidden behind a curtain of the more obvious criminals, and behind regulations that benefit the few at the cost of the many.

Any social organization based upon fear and domination that devalues and disempowers the individual can only produce atrocities: violence, terrorism, torture, the theft of native lands, the destruction of indigenous cultures, the enslavement of whole peoples, the wholesale exploitation and destruction of the environment, the extinction of species, and the quashing of individuality.[1]

The Elephant in the Living Room

The Matrix of the materialists is based in duality; to unravel the code of the Matrix, we have to understand not only how duality works, but how we can make it work for us.

In physics, as in life, we evaluate and compare: we categorize everything in terms of quantifiable values and known qualities. But at the subatomic, quantum

---

1 "Unplug From the Matrix: Truth is Sometimes Stranger Than Fiction"

level, all the rules suddenly change. When scientists discovered that their expectations changed the outcome of their experiments, it implied that at the quantum level, the witness and the witnessed—cause and effect are "entangled." Quantum physics is devastating in its implications because it calls into question the validity of empirical evidence, and the nature of the observer and the observed.

When the underlying nature of reality is explored at the quantum level, the resulting theories have nothing to do with separate entities, and everything to do with a mysterious, implied Oneness or unity. In Oneness, cause and effect cannot exist because nothing is separate. There is no valuation or spatial orientation; no up or down, no right or wrong, no better or worse.

Quantum physicist David Bohm sought to understand the nature of wholeness, while his colleagues kept on trying to dissect matter into ever smaller parts. He posed the question: What if everything in the visible universe is supported by a larger unseen force?

He theorized that reality is reliant upon an unseen but potent power called the implicate order that underlies and supports the external world of appearances. He describes a force that, like the world of Alice in Wonderland, is fluid and dreamlike; it is unmanifested, godlike, inscrutable, and unknown. The implicate order can be thought of as an infinitely deep and broad sea of potential, while physical manifestation—the explicate—is just a ripple on the surface of that sea. Quantum theory suggests that a presence—a vast consciousness—is behind everything.

> *The stream of knowledge is heading toward a non-mechanical reality; the universe begins to look more like a great thought than like a great machine. Mind no longer appears to be an accidental intruder into the realm of matter, we ought rather hail it as the creator and governor of the realm of matter.[1]*

The Creation of Duality

To create Duality, Oneness had to first imagine a "separate space," so it turned inward and created a bubble inside itself, where the rules of Oneness are temporarily suspended and a new set of rules can prevail. Duality is a playground for consciousness to experiment with the densest form of itself—matter. In Oneness, creativity, as we know it, cannot exist; Oneness is static, Duality is not.

> *Dimly remembered through what you would call history, there was a state of agony in which the powers of creativity and existence were known, but the ways to produce them were not known. All That Is existed in a state of being, but without the means to find expression for Its being. All*

---

1 Sir James Jeans

That Is had to learn this lesson, and could not be taught.

From this agony, creativity was originally drawn, and its reflection is still seen. All That Is retains the memory of that state, and it serves as a constant impetus toward renewed creativity. Desire, wish and expectation, therefore, rule all actions and are the basis for all realities. Within the dreams of All That Is, potential beings had consciousness before any beginning as you know it.[1]

Balancing the Equation

The binary system at the core of even the most powerful computer reflects the simple nature of duality—it is an equation, nothing more. Like any equation, duality is always seeking equilibrium. Without the constant delicate balance of opposing forces, duality collapses back into the primordial state of the implicate.

A pendulum that swings wildly is just as balanced as one that hardly swings at all. The extreme oscillations while we transition from a lower state to a higher one will eventually quiet down to a slow, peaceful swing; each side of the equation will become lighter and less extreme.

An Amusement Park World

This world is like an amusement park. All the rides are here: the Roller Coaster of Emotions, the Ferris Wheel

---

1 "The Seth Material." Roberts, Jane. Bantam. 1976.

of Drama, the Merry-go-round of Karma, and the Ego's House of Mirrors.

In order to enter the park, we had to pay a rather unusual admission fee: we had to forget that we are unlimited, for this is the only way to experience the emotions of limitation: the thrill of fear and the heartbreak of separation.

The Toltecs call the game of duality, the "smoky mirror." We don't realize that we are generating the image in the mirror, and that it is us. The "smokiness" is induced by the parameters of the game; our amnesia is produced by the density and slowness of the space-time continuum.

Duality works on a basic, impersonal principal of reflection (the MOON symbols in the High Priestess card). The goddess Isis in this image shows her perfect reflection. She perfectly reflects us; she mirrors back our consciousness. In Her mirror, we see either darkly or clearly. She shows us either the "smoky mirror" of our reactive thoughts and unconscious emotions or the clear reflection of our innate divinity.

The mirror is "smoky" only when we cloud it with unconscious thoughts and negative, reactive emotions; it is smoky because we don't see the connection between what we witness and what we have thought or felt. The quantum implicate—Source/the quantum field—creates whatever we are prepared to see; She creates reality according to how we command Her. Her body is the reflection that we see in everything around us and in our very physical bodies.[1]

Your Dogma Bit My Karma

Karma is the law of equilibrium seeking to resolve itself over time. The resistance of density and negative emotions "creates" more time. Resistance increases the time lag between cause and effect. This becomes a problem when we can't see the relationship between what we think and what we experience; we forget that as conscious beings, we are both cause and effect. The Matrix uses the time-lag effect of duality to keep us asleep to our own creative power; it uses the belief system and emotional output of the collective consciousness to create and recreate itself.

As you increase your consciousness, you decrease time and things "speed up." In a system of higher vibration, karma is not possible, since without the buffer of time, the results of your actions are realized instantaneously; your thoughts are manifest as you think them.

Like a car wreck, effect crashes into cause, and the old timeline collapses. It is not possible for anyone to want to commit crimes or have ill-thoughts at all, since the effects of the cause they send out (their thoughts / emotions) come back immediately like a boomerang.

1 "The Tarot Key, Unlock the Secrets of Your Soul"

Reality as Idea Construction

We are individualized portions of energy, materialized within physical existence, to learn to form ideas from energy, and make them physical (this is idea construction). We project ideas into an object, so that we can deal with it. But the object is the thought, materialized.

This physical representation of idea permits us to learn the difference between the "I" who thinks and the thought. Idea construction teaches the "I" what it is, by showing it its own products in a physical manner.

We learn by viewing our own creations, in other words. We learn the power and effects of ideas by changing them into physical realities; and we learn responsibility in the use of creative energy.[1]

Energy to Matter Conversion Machines

Consensual reality is an agreement that requires the collective support of a great deal of minds. We energize the system individually and collectively through our internal dialogue. As we describe and define reality to ourselves, the Matrix automatically creates a hologram to mirror the vibrational tone of our thoughts.

---

1 "The Seth Material." Roberts, Jane. Bantam. 1976.

The Matrix is fueled by emotions generated from beliefs that it has programmed into us. As long as we are not aware, we create a world that matches our social conditioning. We are "energy to matter conversion machines" stamping out ideas into objects like automatic 3D printers.

Most of our beliefs are inherited, however they have been rendered invisible to us by the propaganda of the slow-moving social agreement. We do not realize how many of these thoughts and beliefs are around us, forming what we see. Like a fish swimming in the ocean, we accept the water without thinking about it.

Until we wake up to the larger reality, the water will be invisible to us and we will swim in the default direction of the social agreement, not knowing that it can support our thoughts and be at our creative command. Like lemmings in their rush over a cliff, we don't realize that we have a choice to turn in a different direction, and be free.

When we are forced into the left brain by our conditioning, we find ourselves in an artificial world; full-time residents of the Matrix. We are outside creation, separated by our beliefs from the natural world.

The unconscious nature of our beliefs forces us to view nature as separate from ourselves; we can no longer see how we affect what we experience. The limitations of the unnatural separation of right brain from left renders us disempowered and irresponsible at the same time.[1]

A Building of Many Levels
A building with several floors can be a metaphor for various levels of consciousness. The floor of each stage in the building is a one-way glass that permits vision in only one direction—down.

An individual stands on the floor that matches his awareness. Above him is the ceiling of his beliefs; below him are the levels of understanding that he has already gained. The floor is transparent, but the ceiling is opaque: he can see down but not up. He stays on the floor— the frequency zone—that corresponds to his level of awareness. On a lower level, he can only intuit what a higher level may be like; he can only go to a higher floor when he gains knowledge and achieves that matching perspective. Consciousness itself defines the dimension that it "lives" on.

The Creative Belief
We are subject to a habit of thought that forms our reality. This is called a belief. As a rock creates eddies in a stream, a belief affects the source energy that swirls around it.

The mind identifies, not with the Self, but with the clothing of its beliefs. If we lose a belief, the mind races to

---

1 "Unplug From the Matrix: Truth is Sometimes Stranger Than Fiction"

replace it with another. We mistake the camouflage of our beliefs for the reality of who we really are.

Beliefs are very creative. Beliefs call up the power of consciousness to transfer a potential held in the quantum soup of the implicate—unexpressed potential—over to the side of expressed consciousness—manifestation into form. This is why beliefs have to be questioned by every person who seriously aspires to full conscious awareness—especially if the belief did not come from one's own experience but from our social conditioning. Another term for belief could be "limitation," for each belief represents a ceiling to our conscious awareness, and it has to be surpassed in order to advance to the next level.[1]

The Weird Fifth Dimension

Just as the third dimension may be incomprehensible to an inhabitant of the second dimension, a higher dimension is very difficult for us to understand, because our minds are conditioned to a linear perspective of comfortable absolutes.

Imagine that you are standing in a room with two mirrors, each on an opposing wall: you see an infinite number of reflections of your image apparently stretching

---

1 "Unplug From the Matrix: Truth is Sometimes Stranger Than Fiction"

around the world in each direction. This is a metaphor for a singular timeline representing the 4th dimension.

Now, add a couple more facing mirrors on the other walls, and imagine that each of those instances of you from the first timeline represents a real potential you that is now reflected on its own timeline in the new mirrors; this is perception from the 5th dimensional perspective.

Our consciousness in this dimension may be constrained by our conception of linear timelines and absolutes, but a higher dimensional being may see an incalculable number of potentials instead.

The fifth dimension could be called a "probability space," which allows change in more than one direction; causality can move backwards as well as forwards, meaning that you can change the past as well as the future. Some theorists speculate that we are already in the 5th dimension.

> *...we are really not in the third or even the fourth dimension. Our now is a moving point within the 5th dimensional probability space. And I believe that the more that people embrace this idea, the deeper their understanding of our reality will become.*[1]

---

1 "Imagining the TENTH Dimension: a new way of thinking about time and space." Bryanton, Rob. Trafford Publishing. 2006.

Interstellar

In 2014, a film named *Interstellar* explored the possibility of a fifth dimension. In the movie, a future version of humanity that has evolved to higher consciousness comes "back" to save us. These 5th dimensional beings can see all points of time, and want to somehow convey their higher perspective to the protagonist, Cooper.

They know that once he is within 5D, he will be able to go to the exact point in time to give his daughter critical information on how to save the Earth. Cooper sees the bookcase in his daughter's bedroom as a tesseract (four-dimensional hypercube) which shows him a kaleidoscope of potential instances, all in the same space:

TARS: Somewhere, in their fifth dimension, they...saved us.

Cooper: Who the hell is they? Why would they want to help us, huh?

TARS: I don't know, but they constructed this three-dimensional space inside of their five-dimensional reality to allow you to understand it.

Cooper: Well, it ain't working.

TARS: Yes it is! You've seen that time is represented here as a physical dimension! You've worked out that you can exert a force across space-time!

Cooper: Gravity. To send a message.[1]

The Birth of Matter

The universe is a cosmic dance of energy and form: Spirit twirls clockwise to form Matter, and Matter rotates counterclockwise as it dissolves back into energy. Matter—the precious, short-lived particle that exists in the eternal and fleeting moment of Now—hurtles through the illusion of space like an astronaut in a capsule.

Frozen Thought

The material realm is a way to freeze thought into form, objectify it, and allow it to exist in time and space as a separate object. As beings who are capable of "throwing" thought around in this manner, we needed an experimental space, a bubble reality that has the proper conditions for our experiment in consciousness. The danger has always been that we might lose our sense of our true self as we subject ourselves to the conditions of the experiment.

Playing With Omniscience

Consider the idea that your consciousness was present at the beginning of the universe, and that you are so vast that you know everything that there is to know. You are large and small at the same time. You are the creator and the created: in the same moment you are the Sun in the sky and a single molecule of water in the ocean.

Consider that the you that you think of as you is just an idea birthed in the mind of a larger You. And consider that perhaps the smaller version of you has been released as a scout to explore the unique properties of consciousness frozen in the density of matter.

And now consider that you are a god who has forgotten that he created the world he lives in. For some obscure reason, You allowed yourself to become a slave to your own creation.

Your Higher Self

The Higher Self is the larger part of you, the part that could not come into this bubble reality. Let's say that its energy was too big; its frequency was too high. Like trying to fit an adult foot into a child's shoe, it could not fit the whole of itself into this dimension.

The physical self is the thought projection of the Higher Self; it projects an image of itself—an earthbound Avatar—into this reality. The Higher Self is the part that remains "outside" the bubble reality of the Matrix. It informs and nurtures you; without it, you would not be able to sustain your life-force.

You are not always in material form, even when you are awake. Where are you? You are with your Higher Self. When you sleep, you spend some time with your Higher

Self. Awake or asleep, you are getting information from it all the time, but many of us can't hear its voice, because our programming drowns it out.

This is what is meant by the phrase, "the quick and the dead," which refers to the unconscious individual as "dead" and conscious beings as "quick" or alive. When you are acting and thinking through the fear-based structure of the Matrix, your emotions make you "dead" to the messages of your Higher Self. When you have surrendered to the greater intent of the Higher Self, you are able to communicate easily with it.

Turning on the Light
When unity splits, it produces form; like a fractal, each part—no matter how small—reflects the whole. Duality is a clever disguise for Oneness. When you can see the design of the fractal—when you can see the whole in the part and the part in the whole, you have achieved the vision and wisdom of a god, who loves everything as he loves himself.

In our culture, negativity has acquired a huge "bad rap." It is the divine feminine; the negative "black" swirl in the yin-yang symbol. The opposite of materialism is not spirituality; it is enlightenment, a higher view that recognizes the unity underlying all material existence. Spirituality seeks outside for a higher being for inspiration, while enlightenment sees inside and knows. An enlightened man accesses his inner vision—insight / intuition— that allows him to understand that Oneness is the source that supplies all systems above it. Life could not exist without the substratum of Oneness that runs like an underground river beneath all manifested reality. An enlightened man simply acknowledges Oneness and holds it in his consciousness while he observes life in all its diversity: he sees "the divinity in duality."

The Fully Interactive Human

Up until the emergence of interactive media at end of the 20th century, our consciousness was constrained to a virtual two-dimensional perspective by the idea of "story," a linear timeline with an established beginning, middle, and end. Stories and dramas from news, radio, and television programs sent a rigid, singular "truth," "story," or "history" to the masses; they inserted an approved storyline in the minds of the populace, and repeated it on every front. The mass hypnosis of the media is the real power behind the Matrix.

Interactive media, which emerged from a fledgling concept to a full-fledged industry in the space of a few years, has changed the way people think. The main difference between a story and an interactive interface is choice. Interactive design creates intersections in a computer program: places where the user can branch to other choices. Even if he "plays" the interface many times, the "story" can always have a different ending. When both the story and the outcome can be determined by the individual, it triggers a massive change in our consciousness; we become aware, at a subconscious level, of our power to change.

The advent of social media changed the landscape even further; everyone gained a voice and personal platform. The Matrix lost more control, as social media ate away at the very base of its propaganda program. More and more people stopped ingesting the "news" and relied increasingly on the perspectives of their peers to help them describe and redefine the world. Social media taught us three major things: that we have the right and the power to express ourselves; that there are others who think like us; and that collectively, we can make deep changes in the social landscape.

Interactive media changed society in a deep, subliminal way; it inserted the idea of the power of individual choice at such a fundamental level that it has provided us a way to escape the Matrix. It introduced the concept that multiple realities or parallel timelines run alongside one another; it implies that we can choose a different future.

There are a thousand things which prevent a man from awakening, which keep him in the power of his dreams. In order to act consciously with the intention of awakening, it is necessary to know the nature of the forces which keep man in a state of sleep.

First of all it must be realized that the sleep in which man exists is not normal but hypnotic sleep. Man is hypnotized and this hypnotic state is continually maintained and strengthened in him. One would think that there are forces for whom it is useful and profitable to keep man in a hypnotic state and prevent him from seeing the truth and understanding his position.[1]

Breaking the Spell

Social media has prepared us for community thinking by giving us a way to express our opinions and individuality within a virtual social structure; as we do, we learn that our actions within a community can have consequences (good or bad) and thus we learn transparency.

Social consciousness and transparency is the basis of what I call "natural ethics," which is the code underlying the social structure of any real community. Our technology has prepared us for a new, more empowered system as collectively, we begin to imagine a different future. We are poised to break the spell of the Matrix.

---

1 G. I. Gurdjieff

Chapter III

Christ Consciousness

~ 33 ~

Jake Sully: She talks about a network of energy that flows through all living things. She says that the energy is only borrowed; one day you have to give it back.

Love and the Beloved

Evolution is the passage of consciousness through the abstraction of time. Like a seed planted in the fertile ground of duality, awareness grows from the experience of separation. The flower of evolution is the individual, and the nectar of the flower is self-awareness. Infinite Mind returns as a bee to drink the nectar and pollinate the plant, and so the spiral of creation continues to expand.

Everything in creation is programmed with at least a small amount of resistance. Resistance creates time; time allows experience; experience fuels evolution. If some form of resistance were not present, everything would follow its primal and powerful desire—drawn like a moth to a flame—to dissolve back into Oneness. In man, fear has developed to help us resist that pull and stay in the physical; it stops us at the edge of the powerful vortex—the event horizon—of the Beloved.

Evolution is a mandate that drives all creation to grow and expand, and eventually to flower as self-awareness. The journey from a one-celled creature in the primordial soup to a full-fledged god-being is long and difficult; we fight to remember our true nature as we pass through the amnesia of density. The last few steps are the most perilous, as we struggle to shake off the illusion of the Matrix.

Death is not our core fear. We are afraid that we will lose our hard-won consciousness. Fear is the "gravity" that keeps us from leaving the game of density too soon.

Emotions as Creative Tools

Resistance creates stability while desire accelerates change. We can use emotions to control the speed of our experience; fear slows it down, while desire speeds it up.

> NEGATIVE: Resistance / Emotions = More Time (slower) = Heavier = Stability
>
> POSITIVE: Desire / Feelings = Less Time (faster) = Lighter = Change

Emotions are frequency. The scale below rates emotions from the heaviest, Fear, to the lightest, Joy.[1]

---

1 Source: Abraham / Esther Hicks

1. Joy / Appreciation / Freedom / Love
2. Passion
3. Enthusiasm / Eagerness / Happiness
4. Positive Expectation / Belief
5. Optimism
6. Hopefulness
7. Contentment
8. Boredom
9. Pessimism
10. Frustration / Irritation / Impatience
11. Overwhelment
12. Disappointment
13. Doubt
14. Worry
15. Blame
16. Discouragement
17. Anger
18. Revenge
19. Hatred / Rage
20. Jealousy
21. Insecurity / Guilt / Unworthiness
22. Fear / Depression / Despair / Powerlessness

As we ascend in consciousness, we move up the emotional scale; the movement, like an incoming tide, slowly advances over time, erasing the evidence of the waves as it goes. The higher consciousness of the New Earth is defined by positive emotions.

In the scale above, the shift to the new paradigm starts at number seven—contentment. The lower two thirds of the scale will be eventually out of range, and disappear from our experience.

The Prime Directive

The mission of the Higher Self is paramount. You can manifest only when your personal desires are aligned with the plan of your Higher Self.

The process of transmuting a lower density reality into a higher density one involves conscious intent and alignment between the duality-based self with the Higher Self. As we align our personal desires with the intent of our Higher Self, we achieve perfect communication, equality, and partnership with it. Spirit is ready to be integrated into the body of matter—for all the parts of man to come into perfect harmony and partnership with each other.

Card #7, The Chariot

> *This image pictures the Higher Self as the Charioteer whose goal is to descend more fully into material form, represented by the chariot— the physical body. The Chariot on this card is the personal "Merkaba," the body which you have prepared to use as the vehicle for your Soul on Earth.*
>
> *In Ancient Egypt, the word "Merkaba" was actually constructed from three smaller words:*

MER meant a "rotating light," KA signified "Spirit," and BA signified the human body. The Merkaba is the vehicle of ascension; esoterically, it is the process wherein the physical body is transformed into a vehicle for Spirit.

Alternatively, the Merkaba can be seen as the "energy body"—or Spiritual body that resides in all forms. In the human being, it can be "remembered" and thus activated, or rather reactivated. The Star Tetrahedron, also known as "The Star of David" is the sacred geometrical form that is the Merkaba. It is comprised of two opposing tetrahedrons that are spinning in opposite directions.

As the body "ascends" in frequency, the Spirit can "descend" into physical form; thus the two meet in the middle, at the level of the (high) heart. The key to the ascension process is not the mind, or the beliefs, or even the emotions of the aspirant, but the heart.

The "high heart" is the fourth chakra. The fourth chakra stands in the middle of the body chakras; on the physical body, this chakra is the thymus gland. Its function is to bridge the higher chakras with the lower chakras.

The Merkaba, as the "vehicle" of ascension is a way for the timeless, formless, limitless Spirit to enter the experience of limitation, otherwise known as 3D or physical existence. When Spirit first came into human form on Earth, it experienced amnesia, and became crucified on the cross of Space-Time, as pictured in the preceding card, The Hanged Man/REVERSAL.

The act of ascension restores the original MEMORY of divinity (Key #2) and INTUITION (Key #5); the combination of these two principles of consciousness returns the number Seven—the Chariot.

The process of the transmutation of energy to matter—the reciprocal movement of implicate to explicate and back again—is constantly at play in the created universe, but the challenge is to awaken Spirit in Matter, to awaken consciousness inside the dream of material existence.[1]

From Trauma to Trust

If you had a child that had been traumatized, you would not be able to convince him that the world is safe. Collectively, humanity is at this point; we have been traumatized by our descent into the darkness of fear and separation.

Love is not an emotion; it is a feeling, a kind of knowing, a sense of security. Emotions are conditional, feelings are unconditional. Emotions belong to a lower consciousness, and feelings come from a higher consciousness. Something has to precede love, to set the stage, so to speak, so Love can arrive; we must leave the limitation of thought and enter the wide-open space of intuition and feeling. The feeling that must precede Love is Trust. Trust opens the Heart so it can receive Love.

The World as a Description
Some years ago, I had a sudden insight. It fell into my mind one day, like a leaf falling into the still water of a lake:

> *"What if life is not a battle, but a love story?"*

This deceptively simple question changed everything.

The Matrix keeps us in a constant state of war with ourselves and with each other. Freedom, the goal of all those who seek higher awareness, can't be gained in battle—freedom can only come from self-love. Self-love is unconditional. You don't love yourself because of what you do, what you know, or even because of who you are; you love yourself as God does: for the mere fact of your existence. No one can give you freedom; you have to earn it. Not by battling, not by hard work; freedom can be obtained only by surrendering.

The Paradox of Surrender
Love is the mother energy that surrounds, supports, and maintains all dimensions and all physical reality. Like a current of light it pushes against every barrier, seeps through our closed eyes, flows around and caresses our

physical form. It is present in every atom. But as long as we believe in the illusion of separation, we stand like impassive stones in the stream of Love.

The Ego-Mind fights to survive on a planet that demands all the power that it has just to stay in one place. It experiences separation as abandonment. It has no concept of a Higher Self, and feels lost and alone. The Ego sees everything in terms of fighting, survival and domination.

Only when the Mind is willing to accept the Heart as its partner, and let go of the need to survive and protect the physical self, can a full reversal of the misguided hierarchy of domination and suffering occur. The Heart must forgive the Mind and give it Love. Without Love, the Mind cannot take the leap of faith and enter into divinity, for Love is what it craves.

The moment of surrender feels like a fall upwards. The Soul experiences an epiphany. It releases the ballast of negativity. Since it is buoyant—literally "lighter than air"—the Soul naturally rises.

Prosperity Consciousness
We have come to believe that we are limited. Surrounded by an undeniable natural abundance, we close our eyes and believe in the absence of it. As the "lower self" ascends by clearing fear/resistance from its field, more of the Higher Self can descend into—inhabit—the body and mind.

A new sense of security and trust comes to the fore, as fear and survival-based thinking disappears.

Your resonance is your reality; you attract whatever matches the frequency of your vibration. Prosperity is the natural state of higher consciousness. Your Higher Self has never experienced lack, so when it merges with you, lack isn't possible anymore.

Transcendence

In the film *Interstellar*, Dr. Brand explains that love is a force that can transcend the barriers between realities.

Brand: So listen to me when I say that love isn't something that we invented. It's...observable, powerful. It has to mean something.

Cooper: Love has meaning, yes. Social utility, social bonding, child rearing...

Brand: Maybe it means something more— something we can't yet understand. Maybe it's some evidence, some artifact of a higher dimension that we can't consciously perceive. Love is the one thing we're capable of perceiving that transcends dimensions of time and space. Maybe we should trust that, even if we can't understand it.[1]

---

1 *Interstellar* (2014)

Frequency Shift

The buffer of time is slowly dissolving. Time is disappearing or "speeding up" as we collectively move closer and closer to understanding a higher order of consciousness.

We took a long journey through the dense realm of the lower dimensions and now we return "home" with the memory of our experience. When man remembers that the true nature of the universe is Love, he gains the perspective of a Creator god. Rather than longing to "go home" to the Beloved, he becomes the body of the Beloved—Love manifest in the physical world.

Heaven on Earth will come because we have made it so. As we return to our natural state of creative empowerment, we become the living embodiments of Love in Action. At the moment when we recall the Divinity in all things, seen and unseen, we can feel an unseen third element—this is the gateway, the portal to alignment. The bridge between dimensions is Love itself.

Love as the Only Response

Christ, when he admonished his followers to "turn the other cheek," was advocating love as the answer to everything. More than that, he was showing us that it is possible, by maintaining a state of love in the face of negativity, to raise the vibration of everyone around you.

When you have an inclusive, holistic view, you cannot experience fear because your view includes rather than excludes. It is only in exclusion that fear can exist, since you are in a state of separation. This process is a necessary step in the evolution of consciousness.

Collectively, humanity is at a stage of evolution that is called "individuation" in psychology: a stage of childhood when the child realizes he is separate from the world around him. The child, realizing that his body is independent from the body of his mother, forms his individual preferences, and creates an identity from them.

We start in Oneness, in the bliss of wholeness. Then we travel through the darkness of separation and loss. Finally, we are to return to Oneness, but this is not a full return to an undifferentiated state; we carry with us the wisdom of our journey: appreciation for uniqueness, for the gift of free will, for individual expression—and see the unity underneath the multiplicity and diversity of form.

Only in separation consciousness can you even imagine doing something cruel to someone else. This is what unity consciousness—Christ Conscious—means. "Truly I say to you, to the extent that you did it to one of these brothers of Mine, even the least of them, you did it to Me." A true god loves each particle of creation equally. This is our path as well: when we can love without conditions, we are at a higher state of consciousness. There is no way that higher vibrational being would ever hurt anyone else, as The Other is Him, and as such, is Divine.

Christ taught us that the path of Love is the only path back to the Garden of Eden.

Chapter IV

Reconstructing Eden

~ 44 ~

Dr. Grace Augustine: Those trees were sacred to the Na'vi in a way you can't imagine. I'm not talking about some kind of pagan voodoo. I'm talking about something real; something measurable in the biology of the forest.

What we think we know is that there is some kind of electrochemical communication between the roots of the trees, like the synapses between neurons. And each tree has ten to the fourth connections to the trees around it. And there are ten to the twelfth trees on Pandora.

It's more connections than the human brain. Get it? It's a network. It's a global network and the Na'vi can access it. They can upload and download data: memories at sites like the one you just destroyed. The wealth of this world isn't in the ground; it's all around us.

Eden as Enlightenment

Eden is a universal ancient archetype that continues to emerge in art all over the world, under different names. In *Avatar*, Pandora is the Eden of the Na'vi, a lush paradise where all life is connected in a living tapestry. "Pandora" is a Greek word that means "the all-gifted" or "the all-giving," a reference to the abundance of Mother Nature. The Na'vi are depicted as an enlightened people who live in perfect harmony with their world.

Eden is more than a place, it is a frequency, a higher level of awareness. Since the outer form is always a reflection of the inner state, when we change our frequency, we experience a reality that corresponds to our new vibration. The structure of the Matrix is based on the lower vibration of fear, Eden is based upon the higher frequency of Love: fear produces constrictive cages of limitation, while Love produces freedom and creative expression. Eden is the natural experience—the home—of the enlightened man who lives in harmony with the planet and with other men. In order to return to Eden, we need to remember our true origins, before the "fall in consciousness." We have to remember Love.

The Prism of Love

Duality is nested inside Oneness like a fetus in the womb. The implicate surrounds and nurtures us, supplying the energy for all material existence. No matter how dense or dark our world becomes, this energy is still there, nurturing and informing us. As our consciousness evolves, we become dimly aware that there is a greater reality outside ours.

Oneness created duality as a bubble of space-time. The wall of the bubble is a prism that splits the pure white light of Love into three rays, colors, or principles when it enters physical reality:

EQUALITY

BLUE: 6th chakra/head/air element. The unifying nature of love.

Equality unifies people without homogenizing individuals or ignoring distinctions. In a civilization with true equality, government is not necessary. A healthy society rules itself.

RESPECT

GREEN: 4th chakra/heart/water element. Love for diversity and difference.

Respect allows for all kinds of diversity. The French say it well: *vive la différence*, meaning "let's celebrate our differences." Respect for diversity recognizes the sovereignty and free will of the individual; it is an expression of love for difference and variety, an understanding of the divinity in duality.

47

UNIVERSAL ABUNDANCE

RED: 1st chakra/root/earth element. Love for and connection with the Earth.

Equal access to resources makes a utopian society possible. When you have everything that you could want, the drive to have more than you need goes away. Only a glutton keeps on eating when he is full. Greed disappears when the survival instinct is superseded by the higher vibrations of generosity and sharing.

Duality's Equation

The self-appointed rulers of the Matrix don't want you to know the following secret: the Matrix takes advantage of the balancing principle of duality, which is a mechanical law, not an ethical one. By keeping people in ignorance of the way reality truly works, the rulers can manipulate the laws of duality to serve themselves and exploit others.

Here is how it works: duality is an equation that must—emphasize must—balance, or the whole system collapses. If you throw a gross thing like obscene wealth on one side of the equation, it needs something of equal weight on the other side, such as abject poverty. But here is the real key:

The two sides of the equation must be equal in weight but not in size.

On a mechanical scale, a tiny piece of lead can balance a huge sack of feathers. The lead is small and dense, while the feathers take up lot of volume; the feathers occupy more space than the lead, but both objects weigh the same. The rulers of the Matrix use the mechanics of duality in order to maintain their position on the top of the pyramid. In their skewed version of duality's equation, the extravagant wealth of one man is balanced by a huge amount of people who are dirt poor: the two sides of the equation are equal in weight but not in size.

In fact, in the Matrix, wealth must be contrasted by poverty or it is not considered wealth. In the Matrix Mind, the concept of universal wealth is illogical; it is a contradiction in terms. This is because valuation is one of the guiding principles that supports the hierarchical system. In the Matrix everyone can't be equally wealthy, somebody has to have more than someone else or the system breaks down.

The controllers manipulate duality by putting extremes on either end of the balance scale. This trick works with power too: one person with great power is balanced by a large disenfranchised populace. The definition of power in the Matrix is "power over." The more people the rulers control, the more power they think they have.

Using the simple mechanics of duality, the rulers of the Matrix have maintained their colossal wealth and power for eons. They constructed a hierarchy that puts them at the top. Then they reinforced their rule with a belief system for the masses—a fiction the rulers created to keep the populace from ever discovering the true nature of reality; this is how they kept the keys to creation for themselves.

All social structures support the Matrix by promoting the same belief system under different guises, guaranteeing that the ignorant, exploited masses continue to look for some *outside* force to save them, never knowing that the power they seek is *within*.

In duality we experience separation—separation from self-knowledge, from the Self, Source, All That Is. This simple fact of existence has been taken to the extreme and exploited by the rulers of the Matrix for personal gain. Their system relies upon the continued ignorance and spiritual immaturity of the populace; the world rulers are betting that you won't see through their machinations.

The Matrix keeps us in ignorance through our beliefs and fears; it tells us that inequality, greed, and exploitation are natural. When we believe that the Earth is a survival-based planet, we fear powerlessness and poverty. As we engage in fear, we reinforce and recreate the Matrix.

All systems can be reduced to a few fundamental principles that guide them and provide stability and structure. The core premises that drive the Matrix are:

> Valuation
> Control
> Profit

Putting the principles of the Matrix into practice results in the following conditions; they may not be in your backyard but you can bet they exist somewhere in the world:

> *Valuation produces Inequality.*
> *Control produces Exploitation.*
> *Profit results in Privation.*

Poverty, exploitation, and starvation are the results of a profit-motivated system that allows some people to benefit from the suffering of others. It might look OK on the surface, but the deeper reality is that everyone is affected, no one is exempt from the karma of lower consciousness.

> *If one person is enslaved, the whole world is enslaved. If one person is hungry, the entire world is hungry.*

When a few people control common resources—when they can drive the valuation of those resources higher by withholding them from the populace—the world experiences scarcity.

Each one of the principles that support the Matrix can be replaced by its polar opposite:

> *Valuation is replaced by Equality.*
> *Control is replaced by Respect.*
> *Profit is replaced by Universal Abundance.*

The old paradigm of control and domination can exist only when the individuals in it remain ignorant of the greater reality of Love. Once a child learns to read, she cannot unlearn it; she reads wherever she goes. In the same way, once the realization of Oneness and connection is reached, you cannot ignore what you know; you spread Oneness and Love to everyone around you. The Matrix crumbles because its energetic support of fear and scarcity is gone.

Eden is Our Inheritance

We can look to the past for a practical model of Eden. Many ancient cultures exhibited philosophies with an emphasis on equality, respect, and shared resources. In earth-based matriarchal cultures all life was considered sacred. This code of behavior was reflected in their social structure.

Ancient Egyptians' ... codices, attributed to the heq of tribal mothers, came down to dynastic times as the Laws of Maa, or Maat: alternative names for the Goddess as Mother of Truth. Even the gods were constrained to live by the Laws of Maat, which were largely benevolent and pacifist, foreshadowing by many centuries the "golden rule" that appeared later in Buddhist, Jewish, and Christian tradition. Some of Maat's laws commanded that no one should cause pain to others, nor make anyone sorrowful, nor steal,

cheat, bear false witness, stir up strife; neither should anyone harm animals, damage fertile land, or befoul waters.

This matriarchal clan system has been called "by far the most successful form that human association has assumed." [1]

The Prophecy Hidden Inside the Archetype

There are many prophesies of the end of the world; regardless of their origin, overall they predict not the end of the Earth, or of man, but the end of the age of materialism. Most Hindus believe that the current era is the Kali Yuga, the last of four Yugas. Each Yuga has seen successive degeneration in the moral order, to the point that in the Kali Yuga quarrel and hypocrisy are the norm. However, the next period is forecast as a time of enlightenment and harmony:

☙ ☙ ☙

After the Kali Yuga is the Satya Yuga, which in the eternal cycle of ages is defined as the first and best Yuga. It is the age of truth and perfection. Humans are gigantic, powerfully built, handsome, honest, youthful, vigorous, erudite and virtuous. There is no agriculture nor mining as the earth yields those riches on its own.

---

1 "The Crone, Woman of Age, Wisdom, and Power," Walker, Barbara. Harper & Row. 1988.

Weather is pleasant and everyone is happy. There is no disease, decrepitude or fear.[1]

Shambala

Shambala is a legendary kingdom in Tibetan Buddhist tradition, sought by Eastern and Western explorers. In the ancient Tibetan scriptures, existence of seven such places is mentioned. Khembalung is one of several beyuls ("hidden lands") believed to have been created by Padmasambhava in the 9th century as idyllic, sacred places of refuge for Buddhists during times of strife.

The ancient texts seem to be talking about a place that actually existed, and possibly still exists. The legend describes a high culture, a vision of man living in harmony with both nature and with his fellow man; a place that is untouched by the greed and decadence of the outer world. Shambala is prophesized to re-emerge after the end of the age of materialism to save the world:

In Tibetan Buddhist and Hindu traditions, Shambala is a mythical kingdom hidden somewhere in Hollow Earth, seen as a Buddhist pure land, a fabulous kingdom whose reality is visionary or spiritual as much as physical or geographic. The legends, teachings and healing practices associated with Shambala are older than any organized religion.

---

1 en.wikipedia.org/wiki/Yuga

Shambala may very well have been an indigenous belief system, an Alti-Hymalian shamanic tradition, absorbed into these other faiths. This pre-existing belief system, also called Mleccha (from Vedic Sanskrit mleccha, meaning "non-Vedic"), and the amazing abilities, wisdom and long life of these 'sun worshipers'—the Siddhi from the Vedic Sanskrit—is documented in both the Buddhist and Hindu texts.

The name Shambala first appears in a Tibetan text known as the Kalachakra tantra—or Wheel of Time teaching. The Kalachakra doctrine belongs to the highest level of Buddhist Mahayana teaching, and those who follow it can reach enlightenment in just a number of years rather than a whole lifetime."

The kingdom of Shambala preserves the wisdom of humanity, sparing it from the destructions and corruptions of time and history; ready to save the world in its hour of need. The prophecy states that each of its 32 kings will rule for 100 years. As their reigns pass, conditions in the outside world will deteriorate. Men will become obsessed with war and pursue power for its own sake. Materialism will triumph over all spiritual life. But just when the world seems on the brink of total downfall and destruction, the mists will lift to reveal Shambala.[1]

---

1 en.wikipedia.org / wiki / Shangri-La

A Modern Version of an Ancient Legend

The author James Hilton obviously drew inspiration for Shangri-La from the ancient legend of Shambala. His novel *Lost Horizon* has resonated with many people since it was published in 1933: today, the word *Shangri-La* is synonymous with paradise. Hilton's novel takes the archetype of Eden far beyond a simple symbiosis of man and nature. *Lost Horizon* depicts a modern civilization of refined sensibility and high cultural achievements.

Shangri-La is described as a mystical, harmonious civilization, nestled in a valley in the western end of the Kunlun Mountains. The people are almost immortal, living years beyond a normal lifespan and aging very slowly in appearance. The book's protagonist, Conway, is an outsider who is brought to Shangri-La when his plane crashes. At first skeptical, he comes to understand that the philosophy of the inhabitants of Shangri-La is the secret behind their longevity and happiness. He is intrigued by the absence of crime and the lack of laws:

> *[Conway] was particularly interested, as a student of affairs, in the way the valley population was governed; it appeared, on examination, to be a rather loose and elastic autocracy operated from the lamasery with a benevolence that was almost casual. It was certainly an established success, as every descent into that fertile paradise made more evident.*

Conway was puzzled as to the ultimate basis of law and order; there appeared to be neither soldiers nor police, yet surely some provision must be made for the incorrigible?

Chang replied that crime was very rare, partly because only serious things were considered crimes, and partly because every one enjoyed a sufficiency of everything he could reasonably desire. In the last resort the personal servants of the lamasery had power to expel an offender from the valley—though this, which was considered an extreme and dreadful punishment, had only very occasionally to be imposed. But the chief factor in the government of Blue Moon, Chang went on to say, was the inculcation of good manners, which made men feel that certain things were "not done," and that they lost caste by doing them.

"You English inculcate the same feeling," Said Chang, "in your public schools, but not, I fear, in regard to the same things. The inhabitants of our valley, for instance' feel that it is 'not done' to be inhospitable to strangers, to dispute acrimoniously, or to strive for priority amongst one another. The idea of enjoying what your English headmasters call the mimic warfare of the playing-field would seem to them entirely barbarous—indeed, a sheerly wanton stimulation of all the lower instincts."

Conway asked if there were never disputes about women.

"Only very rarely, because it would not be considered good manners to take a woman that another man wanted."

"Supposing somebody wanted her so badly that he didn't care a damn whether it was good manners or not?"

"Then, my dear sir, it would be good manners on the part of the other man to let him have her, and also on the part of the woman to be equally agreeable. You would be surprised, Conway, how the application of a little courtesy all round helps to smooth out these problems."

Certainly during visits to the valley Conway found a spirit of goodwill and contentment that pleased him all the more because he knew that of all the arts that of government has been brought least to perfection. When he made some complimentary remark, however, Chang responded: "Ah, but you see, we believe that to govern perfectly it is necessary to avoid governing too much."

"Yet you don't have any democratic machinery—voting, and so on?"

"Oh, no. Our people would be quite shocked by having to declare that one policy was completely right and another completely wrong."[1]

The Code of Eden

The vitality and happiness of the inhabitants of Shangri-La is due to the application of their philosophy. Note that they do not have laws; instead they have customs. A custom is a code of behavior that originates from the "bottom up"—from the people—while a law originates from the "top down"—from rulers or government. A custom is observed; a law must be enforced: a custom assumes adult behavior, while a law presupposes criminal behavior.

In an enlightened culture, greed, irresponsibility, disrespect are frowned upon and simply "not done," actions exhibiting these traits are considered poor manners. Worse, the character of anyone committing an infraction would be negatively affected: they lose social status in the eyes of their neighbors. In such a society, your reputation is your wealth—you gain status by doing good for others, creating a great work of art, contributing to your community in some way, or by simply being kind.

There is only one law that an enlightened civilization needs: The Golden Rule. This idea is nearly universal:

---

1 "Lost Horizon." Hilton, James. Macmillan. 1933

The Golden Rule or law of reciprocity is the principle of treating others as one would wish to be treated oneself. It is a maxim of altruism seen in many human religions and human cultures. The Golden Rule differs from the maxim of reciprocity captured in "do ut des"—"I give so that you will give in return"—and is rather a unilateral moral commitment to the well-being of the other without the expectation of anything in return.

The concept occurs in some form in nearly every religion and ethical tradition. It can also be explained from the perspectives of psychology, philosophy, sociology, and economics. Psychologically, it involves a person empathizing with others. Philosophically, it involves a person perceiving their neighbor also as "I" or "self." Sociologically, 'love your neighbor as yourself' is applicable between individuals, between groups, and also between individuals and groups. Richard Swift suggests that "without some kind of reciprocity society would no longer be able to exist." [1]

Do not do to others what you would not want them to do to you [is] the single greatest, simplest,

---

and most important moral axiom humanity has ever invented, one which reappears in the writings of almost every culture and religion throughout history, the one we know as the Golden Rule.

Moral directives do not need to be complex or obscure to be worthwhile, and in fact, it is precisely this rule's simplicity which makes it great. It is easy to come up with, easy to understand, and easy to apply, and these three things are the hallmarks of a strong and healthy moral system.

The idea behind it is readily graspable: before performing an action which might harm another person, try to imagine yourself in their position, and consider whether you would want to be the recipient of that action. If you would not want to be in such a position, the other person probably would not either, and so you should not do it.

It is the basic and fundamental human trait of empathy, the ability to vicariously experience how another is feeling, that makes this possible, and it is the principle of empathy by which we should live our lives.[1]

---

1 Adam Lee, Ebon Musings, "A Decalogue for the Modern World"

Natural Ethics

When there are enough people who resonate with the new frequencies, a new matrix is formed, one made of the frequency of love. This matrix will work as a net of support for the entire planet.

When people live in communities that focus on harmony, equality, and inclusion rather than on domination and greed, a new social system naturally emerges based upon what I call "Natural Ethics." Everyone in such a community agrees upon a new basis of consciousness— the qualities of respect, personal sovereignty, inclusion, and shared resources are the norm.

When you are "known" for what you bring to others—your talents, skills, and generosity of spirit—you can relax and grow naturally inside the community of man. There is no desire to commit crimes against others, because you know that what you do unto others is what you do unto you. This is the Golden Rule applied to a social structure. Once the unnatural Matrix based upon greed and fear is removed, the human can return to his natural self. The world becomes a veritable Paradise as we care for the Earth and all upon her.

And should you ever come to question what you want for the future, see how you respond to these words:

Freedom, wholeness, love, equality, co-creation, unity, personal sovereignty, harmony, balance, authenticity, creativity, and interdependence.

If you feel these words as a pure truth in your being, then you are squarely in the vibration of the New Earth. These words are not mere abstract concepts, but full spirit-in-body expressions that are part of a whole new frequency, a whole new future.[1]

The Lateral Organization

Anyone who spends time outside has to marvel at the way that nature organizes to support life. Think of a meadow: each blade of grass is laterally connected to all the other blades of grass through a shared root system.

A Lateral Organization is a grassroots cooperative, a loose association of individuals in which no one is more important or more valued than another. A Lateral Organization is not a hierarchical system; it is more like the round table in King Arthur's day, with equality as the structure and respect for the individual at its core.

A bee hive could be considered a kind of lateral organization but there are crucial differences. In a bee hive, there is equality but no individuals; each bee is defined by their role in the hive and is utterly replaceable. Even the queen can be replaced with another female. The base unit

1 "Unplug From the Matrix: Truth is Sometimes Stranger Than Fiction"

is the worker bee, which is not an individual so much as a role. There are, in fact, only three roles in a bee hive—the worker bee, the drone, and the queen. Each bee is literally worked to death, and then replaced by another bee that functions in the role. The hive doesn't care about an individual bee. Whether a drone or a queen, they are replaceable parts of a machine. The bee society draws its strength from this structure: its purpose is to merely survive, not grow. The intent of the hive is the survival of the hive, not the wellbeing or growth of the individual within it.

In contrast, the Lateral Organization emphasizes the individual, not the role. The wellbeing of the individual is paramount: the organization works only when each member is happy. Equal but different is the rule. Since there is no benefit in gaining power over others, people lead only when it is needed or when it is personally fulfilling. Without a hierarchy of leaders and workers, an individual can be called upon to serve in whatever capacity is required at the time. All roles are temporary, determined by consensus. As the individual develops he / she may pursue different roles for the experience or for their growth, leave the organization, or pursue other life goals. As each person seeks to grow in the way most natural for him or her, the organization and society as a whole benefits.

The New Currency

In elementary architecture, an arch is built of stones that remain together because they all press into the keystone, the central stone at the summit. The keystone is the "key" that locks the whole arch together. If you remove it, the arch crumbles.

> **The key to the Matrix:**
> **"Limited resources controlled by a few."**
>
> **The key to New Eden:**
> **"Universal abundance, shared by all."**

If the underlying intent of a system changes, the whole structure above it is transformed. If we replace competition and greed with cooperation and sharing, we end up with a new paradigm: an enlightened culture. Eden encourages sharing as an expression of its mandate of expansion and flow. The power of Love can infuse money; when it does, it returns money back to its original meaning: a means of exchange between people. No longer dammed with greed, the currency of the planet flows like the natural resource that it represents.

Prosperity is the natural experience of a higher-level being; universal abundance is the fundamental expression of an enlightened people. Money becomes what it should be: a gush of abundance that flows into each nook and cranny of the New Earth, supporting the transition back to a veritable Eden, with plenty for all.

The Return of Eden

Matter and energy is in an eternal dance. Matter, the product of energy, desires to return to an undifferentiated state—back to a state of Oneness. On the other side, energy desires expression in material form. So the dance between the negative-feminine force and the positive-masculine force is endless, since if either completely gained its goals without the balance of the other, the universe of form would fly apart.

Everything that you can think of is a symbol, and the current of your mind carries each symbol as a leaf is carried in a stream. But there is a deeper reality, and that is one of raw energy. And this energy pops in and out of view to the observer as a particle or a wave. Like a vast sea of possibility, with forms created and dissolved, the energy emerges as a rock, a tree, an animal, or as a human, and participates in a complex cooperative synchronicity that we call reality.

Consider that everything, from the grass to the trees to the sightless fish in the deepest cave, is just a concept—one of an infinite number of ideas in a vast consciousness. Everything in the universe manifests at your behest through the alchemy of your unconscious or conscious desire.

Imagine now that you are connected to the Earth and the Earth is connected to you. Even the rocks are alive. The Earth is intelligent: it communicates—communes—with you.

Information and energy passes through you and to you through this connection, as fluids pass from a mother to her baby through the conjoined umbilical cord. The plants, animals, and elements of the Earth are the cells of the planet, and you are its brain.

Humans represent the flowering of consciousness on a planet that is itself in the process of evolving to a higher state. Together, you and the planet are in perfect harmony; you experience through each other. Through the natural interface of your body, you and the planet literally think with one mind.

Chapter V

The Avatars of Eden

~ 55 ~

I see you.

The Earth as Eden

Our legends tell us that Earth was once a paradise for all living beings. Hidden in the mists of time, it is the place of our birth; the physical realization of our natural frequency. After eons in the Matrix, separate from our true nature, from Love, and from everything we know to be true, we long to go home.

The consciousness of the masses holds the base vibration of the planet. To shift our reality, we have to upgrade this frequency. The collective cannot do it because their job is to maintain the status quo. They haven't been trained to create. Only conscious creators can switch the frequency, and turn Earth back into Eden.

The Creative Genius

The creative genius lives outside the Matrix. His mission is change and evolution. The word "genius" comes from the Latin verb *gignere* meaning 'to give birth or bring forth.' It is the creative genius who will give birth to the New Eden.

The social structure of the Matrix is highly resistant to change. It exerts huge pressure on all its members, a compulsion to conform. Most people respond by complying, and don't think to question the status quo. In contrast, the creative genius is a radical thinker. He is the "virus in the body of The Matrix" who, by his very existence, threatens the stability—and, ultimately, the very survival—of the social structure.

————————

The da Vinci Virus

The freethinking individual represents the natural evolution of mankind: this is what the Controllers fear. Throughout history, mankind has been advanced by the individual—not by the state, the religion, or the collective.

None of the groundbreaking ideas that have contributed to the evolution of the species of man has come from the collective, they have come from the individual who thought outside the box of the mass consciousness—outside the limitations and beliefs that comprise the Matrix.

This was often at the cost of their lives.

The individual who has learned to think for himself is like a virus in the body of the Matrix: the white blood cells of the Matrix, disguised as Agent Smith, seek to destroy him. Once you have exited the Matrix you cannot get back in: the Matrix won't let you. And once you have learned the truth it is impossible to forget. You can no longer go back to a lower consciousness, and allow yourself to be enslaved once again.[1]

Back to the Future

The Renaissance was a sudden flowering of human consciousness that began in the 14th century and stretched all the way to the 17th century. It was led by a few educated visionaries.

Most people in the Renaissance were servants or merchants who had no practical use for science, philosophy, or other esoteric pursuits, and did not therefore have the benefit of an advanced education. We can count the creative geniuses of that period on one hand. But those few visionaries brought us out of the Dark Ages, and transformed Western Civilization.

Now we are at the birth of a new Renaissance. Like the movement in the 14th century, it will be led by the creative genius, but this renaissance will be infinitely more powerful. In fact, the current situation looks like the perfect setup for an explosion of awareness and new ideas:

---

1 "Unplug From the Matrix: Truth is Sometimes Stranger Than Fiction"

The Matrix is Exposed
It is obvious that the old system is not here to benefit its constituents. The gap between the haves and the have-nots is widening, the middle class is disappearing into bread lines, and the 99 percent are becoming more vocal with each passing day. Many people are ready for something new.

Communication
We are in a position to reap the rewards of new media. The internet democratizes communication; it accelerates the transference of new ideas, alternative news, and aids global communication.

A Network of Minds
Your neighborhood is not your physical location, but a grouping of like minds in a virtual space. The connections between the members of a group are like the synapses in a huge brain—a single mind that represents a vast number of individuals.

Inborn Talents and Skills
With each successive decade children are born smarter and more connected than the generation before. It seems that they arrive with great talents, skills, and wisdom fully realized. These brilliant children grow into powerful adults, with the capacity to create worlds, and their numbers are growing.

Creative Numbers

There are more creative geniuses on Earth than at any other time in the history of mankind. The sheer pressure of the numbers of creatively empowered people is destroying the Matrix from within.

The Creative Spirit

The creative spirit is spreading globally, infecting many with the virus of freedom; people are starting to demand basic human rights. New leaders in every field are starting to emerge; these people know exactly how to create a new world that will work for everyone.

The Secret Wellspring

Creative visionaries don't create from what they see around them. They access the quantum implicate through their imagination. The creative genius doesn't create out of thin air, he "remembers" a potential from the vast warehouse of the implicate. He knows how to mine the collective conscious and pull from the sea of potential the elements of whatever he desires. Creativity is remembrance. Inspiration for creating new paradigms always comes from "out of this world;" from beyond the system and from beyond the personal experience of the individual.

A visionary sees past the collective agreement, beyond manifested reality, into the vast open space of the imagination. He "remembers" another potential reality, draws it from the quantum implicate, and then feels his way back into it.

The Perfect Storm

Artists use desire as a tool; desire generates power by creating tension and a gap between where one is and where one wants to be. This simple creative principle works the same way on a larger scale. The enormous amount of tension created by the swiftly-widening gap between our desire for a better world and the reality of the Matrix is accelerating the evolution of the planet.

Throughout time, the creative genius worked to bring forward human evolution. We are at the threshold of a pivotal event: a sudden flowering of consciousness. The stage has been set: there are more geniuses on Earth than at any other time in the history of mankind, and the conditions of the planet are the perfect environment for incubating a totally new paradigm.

The repressive system of the Matrix actually encourages the evolution of consciousness. Throughout history, all periods of intense repression are followed by a subsequent burst of creative growth.

In the future, we will look back to the current age as a Dark Age that preceded an incredible renaissance, an explosive growth and evolution, this time in alignment with the planet, and with the good of all at heart.

The Avatars of Eden

Those who came to shift the consciousness of the planet are Avatars. As a higher consciousness in physical form, we require a higher vibrational reality—an Eden—for our home. Our innate energetic signature affects and ultimately transforms Earth.

In Hinduism, an *avatar* is an incarnation in human form; a deliberate descent of a higher form of awareness into a lower physical plane.

AVATAR

1. the incarnation of a deity (such as Vishnu)

2a. an incarnation in human form

2b. an embodiment (as of a concept or philosophy) often in a person [1]

You know you are an Avatar when your ideas, beliefs, and sense of what's right doesn't match the reality system in which you are embedded; they align with a higher order instead. You were dropped into the Matrix by your Higher Self to wait until the time of transformation.

---

1 www.merriam-webster.com/dictionary/avatar

Perhaps you knew of the shift all your life, or maybe it is something that you recently learned. Sometimes you despaired of ever completing your task. The rest of the world seemed to go on, oblivious while the reality shifted and shifted again right under their feet.

For a while, you felt like a modern oracle, predicting futures that no one wants to see. Meanwhile, your personal world fell apart in every way possible, and you were left standing all alone. With nothing left that could possibly engage, amuse or distract you, you waited.

You are in your chrysalis changing, inexorably, at the energetic and cellular levels, for what seems to be eons. Your life shrinks down to the moment: the past seemed to be a dream or someone else's life, a story that becomes less and less plausible without emotional drama. Emptiness is your constant companion. You try to envision the future, but all you see is whiteness: a blank page.

Now you are ready.

Path of Manifestation

We are the creators of the material realm. When a human being is unconscious, he acts like an energy-to-matter conversion machine. And what does the machine-man create? More of the default Matrix, because in man's unconscious state his intent aligns with that of the machine.

A conscious creator knows that his thoughts and emotions affect his environment. He seeks to direct his consciousness towards creating a new Earth. To direct the manifestation process consciously, you have to use intent, which comes from beyond the physical realm. Intent is not a thought, since it has nothing to do with your mental body; it isn't a hope, wish, or prayer, since it is also beyond your emotional body. Intent is a silent knowing that could be said to come from your Higher Self. It is a message or a command that you cannot originate from your mind or your emotions; instead you have to align yourself with the greater intent of your Higher Self.

In order to use intent, you have to go back to the primal force of alignment: your feelings. Each vibrational reality is a feeling in your body. Feelings are not to be confused with emotions. Feelings are pure intent; feelings align worlds. You communicate with your Higher Mind through your feelings. You communicate with your Higher Mind through your feelings — the language of your Soul.

The easiest way to change manifested reality is to influence the process at the inception, when it is at the stage of pure energy. The Matrix has convinced us the only way to change things is to work with the material, but this is false. Not only is it difficult, but this idea forces us to focus our attention on the wrong side of the process. Physical reality is the result of intent, not the reverse. Intent comes from (or through) the Higher Self, which resides outside of what we think of as manifest reality.

When you surrender in the state of inner silence, your command becomes the command of the Higher Self, or, more accurately, your personal intent becomes aligned with that of your Higher Self.

The Lure of the Archetype

Archetypes are a kind of bridge between the fundamental reality of Oneness and the reality of duality. Carl Jung stated that the archetype is not just a psychic entity—it is a power in charge of matter itself.

The Archetype of Eden—the ideal environment for the evolution of man—comes to us from beyond duality, from the field of the implicate, as a mandate and beacon from our Higher Selves. It beckons us towards an empowered future.

>...[An archetype is] a mediator of the unus mundus,[1] organizing not only ideas in the psyche, but also the fundamental principles of matter and energy in the physical world.

>Jung suggested that not only do the archetypal structures govern the behavior of all living organisms, but that they were contiguous with

---

1 Latin for 'one world,' an underlying unified reality from which everything emerges and to which everything returns

structures controlling the behavior of inorganic matter as well. [1]

The Final Step

The Avatar sees through the propaganda of the old Matrix. He is here to shift first his own consciousness and then that of the collective. Throughout his sojourn on Earth he has progressed through different roles, each one part of a larger process or plan:

First, he became an Iconoclast (11), with the drive to expose the lies of the old paradigm, with a mission to tear down the system and wake up the masses. Then he graduated to the next level, and became a Master Builder (22), ready to work together with others in a team to create the new world. Finally, he realized Christ Consciousness (33), and with the knowledge that New Earth is built from the blueprint of Love—he became an Architect of Eden (44).

For each step he made, the Avatar has had to throw away the belief system and knowledge of the step before. As in the metaphor of the building with many floors, when he looks back over his life he realizes that at each stage he couldn't see the floors above him, only the ones below. Each stage was important. Just as the upper floors of the building would collapse without the lower floors supporting them, so each stage of his process became the foundation for the next one.

---

1 en.wikipedia.org/wiki/Jungian_archetypes

Now he is at a critical juncture: he has to let go of everything that brought him here. Only when he is capable of releasing the story of his journey through the Matrix will he will be free. He replaces knowledge with *knowing*, history with *desire*, and time with the *now*.

The conscious creator is a fluid being who exists only in the now. All decisions, knowledge, and goals are experienced, not as things or events in space-time, but as kinds of *intensity*. His personal intent, now aligned perfectly with that of his Higher Self, is the singularity[1] that precedes the flash point of creation.

A Gift From the Cosmos

In Chapter One, I stated that the most basic belief that supports the Matrix is the concept of "Survival of the Fittest." The idea that it is a "dog eat dog" world fits the controllers' scheme perfectly; it keeps the masses in constant battle for resources. But perhaps the most pernicious belief is that man does not have the ability to change himself, much less build a better world. I wrote this book to show that this agreement can be changed.

To shift the consciousness of the planet to another dream, two things have to happen. One of them is energetic and not under our control, the other is mental and is under our control.

---

1 A point at which a function takes an infinite value, especially in space-time when matter is infinitely dense, as at the center of a black hole.

The energetic part is already happening. The planet has been receiving "pulses" of higher and higher frequencies for a while now, originating from the center of the galaxy.

For more than 10 years the H.E.S.S. observatory in Namibia has been mapping the center of our galaxy in very-high-energy gamma rays. These gamma rays are produced by cosmic rays from the innermost region of the galaxy. A detailed analysis of the latest data, published on 16 March 2016 in Nature, reveals for the first time a source of this cosmic radiation at energies never observed before in the Milky Way: the supermassive black hole at the center of the galaxy, likely to accelerate cosmic rays to energies 100 times larger than those achieved at the largest terrestrial particle accelerator, the LHC at CERN.

The center of our galaxy is home to many objects capable of producing cosmic rays of high energy, including, in particular, a supernova remnant, a pulsar wind nebula, and a compact cluster of massive stars. However, "the supermassive black hole located at the center of the galaxy, called Sagittarius A, is the most plausible source of the PeV protons…" [1]

---

1 www.nature.com/nature/journal/v531/n7595/full/nature17147.html

Scientists now suspect that the energy emanating from the center of the galaxy is affecting evolution: in fact, it may be the primary agent. These energies influence every life form on the planet and transform matter itself from the inside out. You cannot hide, and you cannot help but be transformed.

...gamma-ray bursts may cause long-lived changes indirectly by affecting planetary atmospheres. Significant gamma-ray irradiation from supernova explosions are more frequent and have a much longer duration and may be capable of driving evolutionary effects directly. Both of these distant cosmic sources are capable of delivering atmospherically and biologically significant high-energy radiation jolts every hundred thousand or million years -- possibly hundreds or thousands of such events over the history of a planet.[1]

The Dream Team

The Toltec seers claim that we are dreaming one hundred percent of the time. The collective consciousness of humanity is but a dream; one that we can change. This is sometimes called "jumping timelines." While there really isn't such a thing as a "timeline," there is a certain inertia to mass consciousness.

---

1 www.spaceflightnow.com/news/n0201/11radiation/

This inertia maintains a collective agreement that allows us to perceive the same things. Each agreement is a description of reality: we have agreements among our family members, agreements that pertain to our communities, to our nations, and to the human experience itself. Established by our relationships, they are like circles within circles; collectively, our agreements maintain our description of reality.

The Avatar dares to dream a different dream. He joins with other creative visionaries: together, they pressure the collective, and the paradigm shifts accordingly.

The dream universe possesses concepts which will someday completely transform the physical world, but the denial of such concepts as possibilities delays their emergence.

There are also shared or "mass" dreams. In these mankind deals with problems of his political and social structure. In these man dreams individually and collectively of ways in which changes could occur. These dreams actually help bring about the resulting change. The very energy and direction of these dreams will help change the situation.[1]

---

1 "Seth, Dreams and Projection of Consciousness." Roberts, Jane. New Awareness Network. 1998

Conscious Dreaming

In the esoteric practice of lucid dreaming, one must "wake up" in the dream, and know that one is dreaming. Then you can control the dream: fly, go through walls, even change the dream itself. The first step in lucid dreaming is to remember to check to see if you are dreaming.

This is difficult because we tend to always accept that the reality we are experiencing—dream or not—is real. So you are always surprised when you check and discover that you are, in fact, sleeping. However, the hardest part of lucid dreaming is to *stay awake* in the dream. The mind is easily distracted by what its experience and lulled back to sleep.

The real purpose of lucid dreaming is to wake up in the dream of life; to become lucid in daily awareness—to realize that you have the power to change your reality by changing the dream. As in *dreaming*, you have to remember to do the following:

1. Realize you are in a dream.
2. Stay awake.
3. Hold the intent for a different dream.

The Avatar is awake in a way that the populace and even the controllers cannot replicate: he is in a state of constant conscious dreaming. Like the pilot of a ship far out at sea, he keeps his attention sharp while guiding the ship towards the land that no one can see but that he knows is there. The Avatar's focused intent holds the energy that creates the new Matrix of Eden: a grid of energy that surrounds us and supports the web of creation on Earth.

Directed, focused intent, maintained consistently and persistently over "time" always trumps any default intent. The deliberate dreaming of the planet's conscious creators—the Avatars of Eden—helps to speed up the collective's transformation and to buffer it from becoming too abrupt, directing the process away from the necessity of catastrophic events. The vision held by a few conscious dreamers is guiding the entire collective into a new dream.

The Eden Within

The social structure of the Matrix is heavy and rigid. The Avatars are like icebreakers cutting through the glacier of the Matrix. The ice is breaking up and melting. And just as water is a higher vibrational state than ice, we are rising in frequency.

As we rise, we experience purer frequencies. When we surrender to the purest expressions of Love that flow around and through us, we start to remember what we are: containers of awareness that hold the frequencies that make worlds.

The master number eleven can be reduced to a two, the number of duality. The eleven is a doorway to a new reality, guarded by an angel or goddess who asks: "Are you capable of holding the frequency for a new paradigm—a new Eden—inside you?"

The Law of Vibrational Equality
The law of attraction, which could also be called the law of resonance, works in a simple cause and effect manner. Like attracts like. What you are vibrating is your reality. This is what karma means: that you attract the results that match your vibrations, whether these are conscious or not.

> I refer to this universal principle by the anagram, L.O.V.E. — the Law Of Vibrational Equality, meaning that whatever surrounds you has to be your vibrational equivalent.

Like the old Zen Buddhist adage: to hit the target you have to *be* the arrow *and* the target. The vibrational reality of the object, thought, or event precedes and forms the physical manifestation of it. Eden is a frequency, just like the Matrix.

We all must make one decision. What do we want: the hell of the Matrix, or the heaven of Eden? A conscious creator first finds the frequency of what he wants and then holds that frequency within him. To be in Eden, you have to BE Eden.

The Wheel of Karma
Karma is like a huge rotating wheel. The center of the wheel is stable—it is the focal point, the axis of intent. The wheel spins and creates the world. If you are not at the center you are just one of the effects thrown off by the wheel.

In the Matrix, the intent of the wheel is automatic, machinelike. Like any organism, it desires stability—continuance in its present form. If left alone, the force of inertia sustains the default vibrational reality. The wheel will continue to spin and spin in an eternal, unchanging circle called karma.

You cannot leave the wheel of karma until you have transcended the social agreement at the center of the wheel. The key for personal transcendence is inner silence, attained when you stop your *internal dialogue*— the ongoing chatter of beliefs, ideas, and emotions that pursue us for most of our lives.

A constant companion that whispers stories of fear and limitation in our ears from morning to night, we cannot escape the chatter of our minds as long as we exist in fear, but once fear is gone, our internal dialogue is stilled.

Inner silence is accrued over time; when you accrue enough you reach zero point, the center axis of the wheel. When you are at the center of the wheel, you have become cause and not effect; you have become the creator instead of the created.

The wheel of time is stilled, waiting for your command.

The Vortex of Creation

While karma could be compared to a wheel that spins in a circle, evolution is more like a spiral, and life itself is a vortex. The power that supports all created forms, the vortex imbues the physical with life.

A vortex is a very strong powerful energetic shape that cannot easily be disrupted or changed; it is very stable. The vortex is the shape of our emotions in our energy bodies. When our personal beliefs and emotions are combined with those of others, they form a powerful collective vortex that is hard to change: the social agreement. The social structure of the Matrix is a strong energetic vortex, reinforced by its long history, and by the unconscious collusion of the masses.

The vortex is the force of creation that operates incessantly, creating physical forms and whole reality systems as it spins. You cannot change a vortex from the outside. You can only shift it from the center. We can harness the power of creation by placing ourselves at the central axis; when we reach inner silence we are at that center.

The state of inner silence is a surrender to the moment, a state of acceptance. In absolute stillness you align your mind with the intent of your Higher Mind. The force of that alignment creates new worlds. A single drop of focused intent dropped into the pool of inner silence can change the very fabric of reality.

The Domino Effect
In the Matrix of control, domination and greed, creative energy is channeled into producing things that bring profit to the owners at the top of the corporate food chain. In

addition, the social system suppresses all the alternative channels that might produce positive change. Once these unnatural barriers are removed, anything can be achieved. Creativity, channeled into sustainable ventures with support by the community at large, becomes a veritable flood of change, toppling old, unsustainable institutions.

How can you remove the basis of our value-based Matrix at one blow? By providing everyone in every country, no matter how poor, with the same amount of resources; in fact an infinite supply of resources. The technology for this already exists under different forms, but it has been suppressed by corporate interests. They know that when everyone has equal access to energy, their days of power are over. With this revolutionary technology, you can produce whatever you need by taking advantage of the energy that is freely available in equal, unlimited supply to everyone anywhere on Earth. When equality of resources is reestablished on Earth and no one needs to compete or fight for survival, the paradigm shifts.

The Time of the Creative Genius

Artists are scouts into the unknown; I can say that I have seen the future. I have returned from my journey to tell you that you should not be afraid.

The new paradigm is one of creativity and freedom. We will not have the kind of security that comes from amassing great stores of money, or from building a fortress against unseen enemies. Instead, we will find security in our relationships and the quality of our lives. Our assets will be counted not in cold hard cash, but in the measure of our integrity, in the health of our children and society, in the quality of our goods and services, in the inventiveness of our ideas, in the consistency of our friendships, and in the honesty of our partnerships.

What better time to build that new green business, meet new people, sail around the world, have a child, adopt a baby, take loving care of your elderly parents, start a new career, take up photography, make a movie, climb Mt. Everest, learn to ski, go on a archeological dig, teach reading, found a charity, start a school, go on a vision quest or walkabout, or just sit still and meditate.

The time to do what your heart wants is now, because these days mark the beginning of the end of time: as time accelerates toward the speed of light we will finally run out of time. Soon, we will have finally arrived at the finish line of the now. That day will mark the end of the tyranny of time. No longer will you mark your days with a clock, instead, your day will be as long as you want it to be; instead of marking time, spending time, wasting time, or running out of time, you will be able to make time be whatever you want it to be.

The end of time will come when we finally do whatever makes us most happy, when we are finally here and now. When we follow our hearts, which always tell us true, we become timeless and eternal. And so the paradigm shifts, time ends, and your new life can begin.[1]

Shifting Together

Quantum physicist David Bohm believes that the evolution of consciousness is happening with the participation of everyone on Earth. He says that the individual is the "focus for something beyond mankind." Bohm believes that the individual who has acquired personal power can use their focused intent and intelligence to transform mankind. He says the collective understands the "principle of the consciousness of mankind," but they do not quite have the "energy to reach the whole, to put it all on fire."

Bohm infers that those few individuals who have sloughed off the "pollution of the ages" and who understand the principles of love and trust, now have the power to bring mankind into a whole new level of consciousness. These enlightened individuals are those who are more fully in contact with the pure intention at the heart of the Implicate Order, where he states, there is a "consciousness, deep down—of the whole of mankind." At the level of consciousness that sees the connection and indivisibility of things, the directed focus or sustained intent of a few individuals can shift the reality of the entire collective.

---

1 "Celestial Journey: The Voyage of the Creative Spirit"

The natural course of evolution creates ever more complex and sophisticated consciousness. We are witness to a momentous event: the birth of a new kind of awareness, a man who can perceive duality and Oneness at once, and hold them simultaneously in his mind. Enough Avatars with the activated memory and vision of an empowered future is all that is needed to shift the Earth into the Eden it once was and is destined to be.

We stand at the threshold of the most powerful leap in human evolution: this leap will not be physical or technological—it will be a quantum leap in consciousness. There's no one on this planet who did not come to participate in this event. As we evolve to higher consciousness, the underlying nature of the universe—Oneness— requires that everything evolves with us. As we change, so does everything else. Change must happen, because our effort and intention to evolve involves the fabric of consciousness itself.

※ ※ ※

> *As a human being takes part in the process of this totality, he is fundamentally changed in the very activity in which his aim is to change that reality, which is the content of his consciousness. There's nothing else to do—there is no other way out. That is absolutely what has to be done and nothing else can work.*[1]

---

1 David Bohm

A New Currency

A current of water flows freely, restoring and sustaining life wherever it goes. Currency is a symbol for the natural abundance of the Earth, expressed as the energy of Love. No longer dammed by blocks of fear and greed, the current of Love bursts into creative expression on the physical plane.

Humanity's greatest resource is our creativity. We are the Avatars who are here to transform a planet; an empowered society of builders and new world creators who are focused on creating for the common good.

We see the unique beauty and incredible variety of our planet; we know that everything fits together like an intricate and beautiful puzzle.

We know that we are at the center of the intricate web of existence. We rejoice in freedom and would not deny it to anyone. There is a beautiful transparency, and like children, we play in our paradise, as we create and recreate the world each day anew.

The wealth of this planet cannot be measured in precious stones, metals or any material thing. It can only be measured in the courage and drive of the people who are the heart and soul of the planet. Without our creative power supporting it, the Matrix will collapse.

The masses are shifting in their dream state, as the collective consciousness rises to a higher frequency. Eventually, when a crucial tipping point is reached, they will shift to the new direction like a flock of birds, who suddenly turn as one.

The Tree of Souls
We are the Tree of Souls that connects the Earth with the Sky—unified, balanced, in a sacred relationship with each other and with Earth. We are the planet's Avatars who have never forgotten Eden. With our creative genius unleashed, we will bring Heaven to Earth.

The creative impulse comes from the depths of the universe. Born in the quantum implicate, carried across galaxies and vast distances, it emerges as evolution in the field of matter. The same invisible force that fuels the stars and powers the Sun drives us to evolve, and reach for the greater reality of Love.

About the Author

A science fiction addict from childhood, Aliyah Marr was not very surprised to discover a connection between Alice in Wonderland and quantum physics—to her, reality has always been upside-down and backwards. Aliyah lives on the third planet in a yellow dwarf star system about 26,000 miles from the center of the Milky Way galaxy, waiting for the first ship to land.

Aliyah Marr
Creative Consultant for Social Visionaries

www.parallelmindzz.com

Also by Aliyah Marr

The Avatars of Eden
Bringing Heaven to Earth

The Tarot of Creativity
The Oracle of Creative Transformation

The Tarot Key
Unlock the Secrets of Your Soul

Parallel Mind The Art of Creativity
The (missing) Manual for Your Right Brain

The Creative Life in 365 Degrees
Daily Inspiration, Wisdom, Motivation, &
Comfort for the Creative Soul

Celestial Journey
The Voyage of the Creative Spirit

Do It Yourself Tarot
The Instant, Easy Way to Learn How to
Read the Tarot for Yourself and Others

www.parallelmindzz.com

~ Previews ~

UNPLUG from the MATRIX

Truth is Sometimes Stranger Than Fiction

Aliyah Marr

ntroduction

Morpheus: This is your last chance.
After this, there is no turning back.

You take the blue pill—the story ends,
you wake up in your bed and believe
whatever you want to believe.

You take the red pill—you stay in
Wonderland and I show you how
deep the rabbit-hole goes.

The blockbuster movie *The Matrix* was released in 1999. It depicted a bleak future with a simulated reality called "the Matrix," created by sentient machines to exploit humans as an energy resource.

The success of the movie proved that people were ready to hear the truth, even if—or because—it was disguised as science fiction. But truth is stranger than fiction: the Matrix is real—we are living in the Matrix. The following pages read like the script for a science fiction movie, with a cast of malevolent and benign aliens, a league of human minions, a battle for the earth, and an enslaved human populace. Like water pouring down a drain, the Matrix and its supporters are spiraling down to a future of destruction, but not everyone is destined to go down with it.

Many people are ready to jump to a different timeline; to a parallel Earth without pollution, war, exploitation, or power-hungry leaders. If you have always dreamed of a world of equality, opportunity, and abundance, you are ready to make a break for freedom. Once you know the truth, you can never go back.

The key to the door out of the Matrix is in your heart, it has been there all along.

⚰ ⚰ ⚰

Morpheus: The Matrix is everywhere. It is all around us. Even now, in this very room. You can see it when you look out your window or when you turn on your television.

You can feel it when you go to work… when you go to church…when you pay your taxes. It is the world that has been pulled over your eyes to blind you from the truth.

Neo: What truth?

Morpheus: That you are a slave, Neo. Like everyone else you were born into bondage. Into a prison that you cannot taste or see or touch. A prison for your mind.

⚰ ⚰ ⚰

Stranger Than Fiction

Agent Smith: The great Morpheus.
We meet at last.

Morpheus: And you are?

Agent Smith: A Smith. Agent Smith.

Morpheus: You all look the same to me.

The Matrix was the first DVD to sell more than one million copies in the US. By November 10, 2003, the sales of *The Matrix* DVD had exceeded 30 million copies. The movie describes a bleak holographic artificial system that exploits people for their electrical energy. Computer programmer Neo is drawn into a rebellion against the machines, in order to free humanity from the Matrix.

The movie's premise is not too far from the truth, a truth that is initially frightening in its scope and implications. We are in the Matrix, an artificial world that enslaves and exploits us for our energy.

The Matrix is set up to benefit only those few at the top of the pyramid. All exploitation, greed, and life-negating expressions are allowed, while life-affirming expressions are downplayed or even actively discouraged. Those at the top would have you believe that this world is the only world possible; they would have you believe that humans are naturally violent and destructive.

θ θ θ

Unplug From the Matrix reads like the script for a science fiction movie, with a cast of malevolent and benign aliens, a league of human minions, a battle for the earth, and an enslaved human populace. But truth is stranger than fiction—the Matrix is real.

Are you ready to unplug from the Matrix? Once you know the truth, you can never go back.

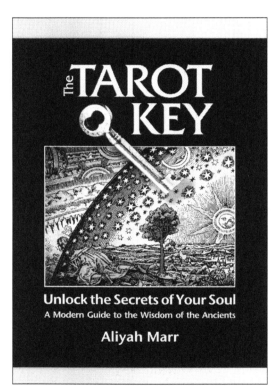

The TAROT KEY

Unlock the Secrets of Your Soul
A Modern Guide to the Wisdom of the Ancients

Aliyah Marr

INTRODUCTION

The Tarot is an ancient tool for self-actualization that gives you to access a vast library of intuitive, innate knowledge that may be otherwise inaccessible to you. From the view of the scientist, you are using the visual side of your brain—the right hemisphere—when you look at the images on the cards. An anthropologist or art historian may see that you are digging into a long-buried treasure house of cultural clues. A psychologist would immediately see the archetypes in the images of the Major Arcana.

The study of the Tarot is a deep probing into the nature of the deeper reality that underlies all things; an attempt to understand that which can never be completely under-stood by the rational brain. The depth and breadth of that knowledge is simply much vaster than the human mind can comprehend. It is our nature to seek a single all-inclusive answer for all the questions that constantly elude us, but failing to find it doesn't stop us from seeking it. The Tarot is the search for the Holy Grail—the well of creativity, wisdom, and personal power that lies within us.

The Tarot is a magical work of art that changes with each viewer, and with each reading. It is a map of human consciousness that is responsive to the degree you are open to what it has to say to you; it teaches you more about you every time you read the cards, even if you read for someone else. Collectively, the cards are an interactive spiritual book of ancient wisdom. Each card is a door to a wealth of information that slowly reveals itself to you over time.

The Tarot asks the same existential and universal questions that mankind has asked since the beginning of time: What is out there beyond our senses? How can we access our true creative power? And how can we understand, align, and create with the forces in our lives?

ONE BOOK FITS ALL

In this book, I show you how to work with two decks: the *Rider Waite Smith Tarot* and with my own deck, *The Tarot of Creativity*. These decks are complimentary; the meaning of each card from one deck adds to the depth of the meaning of the equivalent card in the other deck; however each card system is complete in itself and can be read alone as well.

The Rider Waite Smith deck tends to be very blunt, worldly, and includes some negative interpretations, while *The Tarot of Creativity* is more positive and modern in its titles and interpretations; *The Tarot of Creativity* is designed to provide you with advice even in a negative situation or consequence.

This book was designed to work with any deck. If you are a beginner, you will find it easy to learn to read the cards and develop your own intuition. My revolutionary blended system for reading the cards allows you to pick up any deck and interpret the images instantly. If you are an experienced tarot reader, this book can enhance and deepen your knowledge of the cards.

Introducing the SEER SYSTEM™

In this book, I introduce my system for reading the cards which I call The SEER System;™ it blends four ways of seeing the cards, and rewards the user with instant ways of interpreting the images, numbers, and symbols in each card.[1] It presents a very intuitive way to learn and read the cards.

Dealing From Two Decks

Reading more than one deck at once is called doing a "comparative tarot reading." This technique gives more depth to a reading than possibly can be obtained from one deck. Pioneered by Valerie Sim, the process involves comparing the same card from two or more decks in order to gain additional insight into the card or the spread.

It works best with decks that use the same numbering system, and that are compatible in tone. A comparative tarot reading can be easily done by shuffling and reading from one deck while keeping the other deck in order, so you can pull the corresponding cards from it to enhance your reading.

---

1 The Glossary of Symbols at the back of this book contains a complete list of symbols and their meanings.

111

PARALLEL MIND

The ART of CREATIVITY

the (missing) manual
for your right brain

Aliyah Marr

The best way to make your dreams come true is to wake up"—Paul Valery

INTRODUCTION: THE ADVENTURE OF THE CONSCIOUS CREATIVE

Stories of magic and mystery permeate our cultural history, and have fascinated children and adults for untold generations. Fairy tales and mythologies are full of examples of powerful people who have the ability to generate new objects and realities out of thin air. The archetypical figures in these legends live in our collective consciousness and populate our dreams.

There is a nugget of truth hidden inside these tales. The magicians in these stories are ordinary people who have discovered an incredible power. They know what all of us should know—we are natural magicians. We should know this because it is a truth that is all around us: we modify our environments and create the world in which we live. We are creating our realities all the time. Look around you—it is a self-evident truth. Most of us live in an artificial world of our own construction.

Everything in our man-made environment started out as a creative thought in someone's head. As the idea is caught and visualized, it starts to become more real. The original inspiration becomes denser through focus and concentration, and finally materializes into form.

So someone thinks into existence a chair, a wheel, or a computer. It is the creative thought that forms the eventual material reality. Like a fertilized egg that hatches a chick just because it was kept warm, the actual work of manufacturing the desired object is the inevitable fulfillment of conception. Manifestation is the natural, spontaneous conclusion that follows inspiration.

Creativity is our birthright as human beings. The ironic thing is that we seem to have forgotten our power as creators. We have abandoned our responsibility for our circumstances, and have given our power to remote authorities that do not have our best interests in mind.

When we abandon the responsibility for our development as individuals, we give up a great deal of potential for personal fulfillment and joy. What is at stake is the most important thing to us as individuals and to humankind in general—our evolution.

I guarantee you that you are creative, as we are all creative. The life you are experiencing today is the result of the thoughts you were thinking yesterday. We are holding our reality in existence by our focus on the elements of what we perceive to be our reality. Whether aware of it or not, we are thinking our lives into existence from moment to moment. I propose that if we are creating our lives we might as well be conscious of the process and choose what we want to create.

We are all master magicians; in fact, we are such good magicians that we have deluded ourselves into believing that we are powerless, when in fact, we are the ones in control of our lives. Whether conscious of it or not, we are creating our reality all the time. We are natural creators who have the power to create whatever we want. When we find the power to take control of our thoughts and change our circumstances, we find true independence and creative expression. Nothing is beyond us, because in a state of conscious creation we can live without limits.

However, the average individual feels like a victim of time and circumstance, powerless in the face of what looks like an absolute and insurmountable reality. We are not as helpless as we believe; we are simply unaware of the part we play in our circumstances.

Who can help us regain our power? I have come to understand from my work as an artist that we should look to ourselves for the answers. I know of nothing that has the same potential for self-discovery and empowerment as the process of creating art.

Think about what it would feel like to release the wondrous power that resides within you. What if we are not book making wishes by rubbing a lamp, but instead, we are the Genie granting those wishes to ourselves? Does this idea frighten or excite you?

CHAPTER 1: CREATIVITY

What is your most heartfelt desire? Do you know that you have the power within you to grant any and all of your wishes? Humans are natural creators. It is our birthright to be the creative architects of our lives, not just a leaf in the wind, torn between our duties and our desires.

As humans, we are uniquely gifted magicians—we have the ability to create new things and even modify our environment. Creativity is our talent and our gift, an inheritance from an abundant universe.

Beyond the sense of personal power and control that comes with the practice of art, the fringe benefit is a life filled to the brim with riches. It is impossible to be bored when the world is a playground filled with toys and tools for you to play with and use. Everything is potentially interesting and useful; every event is an opportunity for a learning experience—a spark for a responsive, playful intellect.

Most of my lessons about how to live come from my practice as an artist. I have learned to apply the simplicity and directness of these ideas and found that they work to create whatever I want. I would like to share some of these principles I have discovered with you, so you will be inspired to seek and find your own tools to gain the life that you desire.

The Creative Life in 365 Degrees is a book of daily inspiration for the creative soul. Designed like a calendar book or an oracle card deck, each page contains an inspirational quote for each day of the year. Following are a few sample pages.

DEDICATION

This book is for those who are blessed or cursed with the gift of creative intelligence. Those whose right-brains keep them up at night with brilliant concepts; those who question everything; those who don't respect authority; those who were never understood by their peers, parents or teachers; those who were the class clowns.

You know who you are. You never fit in, were never voted to be famous, and were not popular among your classmates at school. Your parents despaired that you might end up in the gutter because you wanted to be an artist.

You were one of the motley misfits who sat at the back of the room reading science fiction, the art-geek who drew cartoon characters in math class, the budding scientist who experimented with potentially incendiary ingredients from your mother's kitchen in the bathroom, the fledging drummer who just couldn't sit still in grade school.

You were the one couldn't figure out why everyone else wanted to lead a *normal* life. I honor you with our special secret salute (I can't show it here, but you know what that is).

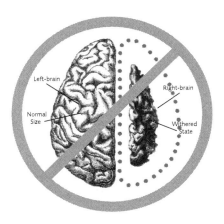

WARNING

The Creative Life in 365 Degrees contains material that may be potentially hazardous for people whose left-brains dominate their lives. If you find inspiration in spreadsheets, tax-guides and statistics then DON'T open this book! You may have an undiagnosed condition that may be aggravated by the concepts inside.

When the left-brain is over-used, it siphons off the blood and starves the creative right brain, resulting in statistical-hysteria and a severe atrophy of your natural creative genius. A brain with this condition will look like the odd walnut with one normal side and one withered side that is said to resemble an uncooked wonton.

The medical term for this condition is "Right brain asphyxia with massive cerebral atrophy" (WONTON). Those with this condition may find this book too stimulating or challenging and may experience unusual symptoms from exposure to creative thinking.

If you decide to read this book anyway, you might experience sudden, irrational, uncontrollable creative desires; you may want to write a book, paint all night, or jam with the musicians next door into the wee hours of the morning. Should you notice bizarre symptoms such as these seek medical attention immediately. Your right brain may be regenerating. Be forewarned: a fully functional right brain can pester you with new ideas, and you may find yourself with a more creative life.

However, if you have a normal or over-developed creative right brain AND know the secret salute, please proceed…

The idea for *The Creative Life in 365 Degrees* was conceived during a short romance I had with Twitter—looking for things to tweet, I started pulling quotes from my book, *Parallel Mind, The Art of Creativity*. I ended up with over 400 quotes that others seemed to find relevant to their creative lives, since they were re-tweeted with regularity during the two years that I squeezed the content of my book through Twitter. I thought it would be fun to put these quotes in a book for artists and designers. A pocket guide full of inspiration for every day of the year; a kind of playful alphabet-soup for the artistic soul.

This book, and *Parallel Mind, The Art of Creativity* are about pure creativity and about the experience of what I call the *conscious creative*, the person who develops themselves consciously—body, mind, and soul—through the practice of their art and through the application of creative thought.

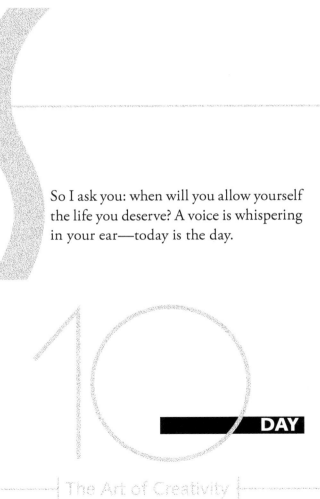

So I ask you: when will you allow yourself
the life you deserve? A voice is whispering
in your ear—today is the day.

DAY

The Art of Creativity

Think about what it would feel like to release the wondrous creative power that resides within you.

DAY 11

Creativity

Did you like this book?

I would appreciate it if you would
post a review via the page below:

http://amzn.to/2dnvnT4

Thank you!

Aliyah Marr